New Perspectives in
Music Theory

"One of the formidable experts and practitioners of jazz and classical music presents a concise and NECESSARY experience in music theory and all its beauty; the basics, very well done. Kudos to Charles Van Riper!"

Bruce Marion
Marion Music
Composer, Author, Musician

"Chuck's book is straightforward and a good read, something I've never experienced in a music theory book in the past 30 years. Reading the book is like sitting down and learning directly from Chuck. It's a must read for anyone interested in the ability to play and understand music without all the "enharmonic equivalent" rhetoric that is common to books on this subject. It provides invaluable insight to the beginning player and (as in my case) "connects the dots" in understanding the "how's and why's" related to music structure, writing and improvisation. I'll never give my copy back, (I have a draft)!!!!!!"

Sean Freeman
Musician's Alliance

New Perspectives in
Music Theory

Charles E. Van Riper

BLUE NOTE BOOKS
FLORIDA

Published by

Blue Note Books
110 Polk Avenue, Suite 3
Cape Canaveral, FL 32920
For additional copies, call 1-800-624-0401

Cover design by Charles E. Van Riper

ISBN: 1-878398-32-6
Library of Congress Catalog Card No. 98-074520

Printed in the United States of America

Acknowledgments

I know nobody reads these things, but in case you happened upon this page, there are a few people without whom this book would never have been possible. Firstly, much thanks to my good friend and killer piano player, Mr. Al Stevens, whose suggestion that I "write it down" got this whole thing started. Secondly, to my wife Becky and my son Harry for their unending patience and love while I was getting this thing together. And wait! There's more! Profuse thanks are in order to Marna Brouchoud, who edited this book so many times she should have it memorized by now, and to Paul Maluccio, our fearless leader and publisher in this project, whose artistry and talents made this whole thing look so dang nice! To all my students and all the teachers I have come to know over the years–see, I told you it works! Finally, much gratitude to all the people, too numerous to mention here, who have graced me with their wisdom, input and support.

Prelude

The original title of this book was going to be "Music Theory Bytes". The first implication here is obvious. The phrase "Music Theory" usually conjures up notions that send most people running for the door. I have found that many of my students put off learning music theory because they thought it was too difficult, like studying quantum physics or the molecular structure of plutonium! Well, I am here to dismiss this myth. Music theory is actually very simple and logical, if you think about it the right way. I have taught this system for more than two decades and found that my students could very easily understand and use the information put forth here in this book. As a matter of fact, the phrase I hear most from my students is "It can't be that easy!", which brings us to the second implication. I have tried to employ as many "short cuts" as possible, many dealing with the material which must be memorized (the key signatures, for example). You could probably just read all the examples and summaries of all the chapters and have a pretty good idea of what's going on. It is essential, however, that you fully understand a section before going to the next. Everything is put together in a logical order, so skipping around will be kind of difficult. Hopefully, this book will give you a simple way to understand chords, scales, intervals, and much, much more. This is also an excellent way to begin understanding the basics of improvisation and composition.

Table of Contents

A Note About Reading Music

(Pun Heavily Intended)

Many of my students ask me if it is really necessary to learn to read music. I tell them well, no it's not, if you don't want to play in a band (any kind of band), learn someone else's tunes, show someone your tunes, communicate at all with other musicians, write your own music, and the list goes on. In other words, if you're content to sit in your living room and play with no one, and doodle around all day, then no, it is not necessary to learn how to read music. However, you will find it MUCH easier to survive in musicland if you do!! I have found that most people think that it is too difficult to learn how to read. WRONG!!!!! As you will see, it is actually very simple. Now, I'm not going to go into a scathing diatribe on reading. Here, we will learn mainly to read the notes on the staff, and that's about it. This is because that is really all you need to know to make it through this book. We will start by looking at the STAFF (those lines that all the little dots are on) and seeing the NAMES of the LINES and SPACES. A music staff has FIVE lines, which creates FOUR spaces. Each line and space has a LETTER NAME that corresponds to a PITCH. Here's what it looks like:

As you can see, each line and space has a letter on it. When a note is placed on the line or space, that is the name of that NOTE. For example, a note placed on the first space (the bottom one on the staff) is called an "F".

It is easy to memorize these letters. Look at the letters on the lines. From the bottom to the top, they are E, G, B, D, and F. Now make up a sentence where each word starts with one of the letters. This is where we get the age old saying: **E**very **G**ood **B**oy **D**oes **F**ine. Use anything you like. JUST MEMORIZE THESE LETTERS!!!

There are innumerable sentences that will do the job if you don't like this one. How about Endorphins Globulate Bucolically Down Front! Well... maybe not that EXACT phrase, but you get the picture. Now let's look at the spaces. The letters of the spaces are F, A, C, and E. They spell the word face, as in "Yo!, music face.....". Well, that was easy enough, eh? Now look at all the notes on the staff:

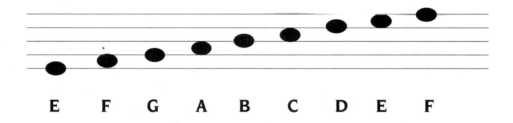

E   F   G   A   B   C   D   E   F

Here we see all the notes going up the staff. They are: E, F, G, A, B, C, D, E, and F. Notice that all the notes go straight up the musical alphabet. (Remember that the musical alphabet goes A, B, C, D, E, F, G, and then starts repeating itself).

These are all the notes that are on the staff, but what about the notes that aren't on the staff (i.e. above or below the staff)? The best way to visualize this is to imagine many lines ABOVE and BELOW the staff. (A few centuries ago, there **were** many lines in the staff. This was called a GRAND STAFF). As we go above or below the staff, the notes would be on an imaginary space or line. Except for the "D" below the staff, and the "G" above the staff, these notes would show these imaginary lines. Let's look at some examples:

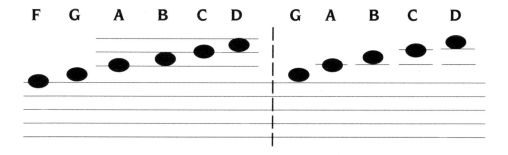

On the left we see what the notes would look like if we imagined the GRAND STAFF, above the five line staff. Notice that the "G" above the staff sits on the top line. On the right, we see how the notes above the staff normally look. Notice that the notes that would be in an imaginary space (the "G","B" and the "D"), do not have staff lines above them, only the lines below them. One way to think of this is: 1 space, 1 line, 2 spaces, 2 lines, 3 spaces, 3 lines, etc. Then just keep going up the musical alphabet, remembering that "G" comes BEFORE "A". These lines that we use to designate notes above (and below) the staff are called LEDGER LINES. We would say, then, that a "D" above the staff has two LEDGER LINES below it.

Well, let's see if we can confuse the matter even more and discuss the notes BELOW the staff. Actually, it's the same as the notes above the staff except for the fact that the ledger lines are above the notes.

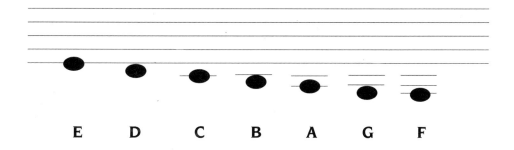

Here are the notes below the staff. Notice that the ledger lines go either through or above the notes and not below them. Except for thinking of the alphabet backwards, this is pretty much the same as the notes above the staff.

Well, that's about it for now, as far as reading music is concerned. As I said before, in order to make it through this book, you only have to know how to read the notes on the staff (and above and below). Hopefully, you now have a little better insight into doing just that. So let's get on with the FUN stuff! What this book is really about... MUSIC THEORY .... and how incredibly easy it can be!!!!!   Have fun and Happy Composing!

Music Symbols

Here are some of the commonly used music symbols you will see.

𝄞	Treble Clef	𝅝	Whole Note
𝄢	Bass Clef	𝅗𝅥	Half Note
♯	Sharp	♩	Quarter Note
♭	Flat	♪	Eighth Note
𝄪	Double Sharp	𝅘𝅥𝅯	Sixteenth Note
♭♭	Double Flat	𝄴	Common Time (4/4)
♮	Natural	𝄵	Cut Time (2/4)
𝄐	Fermata (Hold)	𝄽	Quarter Note Rest
𝄾	Eighth Note Rest	𝄻	Whole Note Rest
𝄼	Half Note Rest		

Chapter 1

The Basics

CHAPTER ONE

The Basics

Music theory is very easy to understand if you can do two things: count to twelve and recite the first seven letters of the alphabet. Let's start with the alphabet. In music, we will be using the following letters: A, B, C, D, E, F, & G. That's all there are! There are no more!! That's all you need to know. All the scales simply keep repeating these letters over and over. In other words, picture this sequence of letters repeating on forever like this: A, B, C, D, E, F, G, A, B, C, D, E, F, G, A, B, C, D, E, F, G, etc. Notice that in this sequence, the letter "G" comes BEFORE the letter "A". Any scale, no matter where you start, will follow this sequence. Then, you merely have to know which notes are SHARP (#), and which notes are FLAT (♭). A SCALE consists of only seven notes. After that, they start repeating in another OCTAVE. For example, if I tell you that there are no sharps and flats in the key of "C", we know the notes in the key of "C" are: C, D, E, F, G, A, and B. After that, we start repeating the same letter names. These will be up in the next OCTAVE.

Before we go any further, let's discuss this SHARP (#) and FLAT (♭) thing. The smallest distance we can have between two notes is called a HALF STEP. This means that there are no other notes between any two notes that are a half step apart. To SHARP a note means to RAISE it, or bring it UP, a half step. Conversely, to FLAT a note, means to LOWER, or bring it DOWN, a half step. For example, let's say that we take a "C" and sharp it. This gives us a "C sharp" or "C#". The distance between these two notes is a HALF STEP. There are no other notes between them. This is the smallest INTERVAL between two notes. An INTERVAL is the distance between two notes. This interval happens naturally in only two places: between "B" and "C", and between "E" and "F". This means that there are no other notes between "B" and "C" or between "E" and "F". All other natural notes may be sharped or flatted. Any note that is sharped (#) is the same PITCH as the note above it being flatted (♭). Are we in deep space yet? Allow me to elucidate. Say we take the note "D" and sharp it to "D#". That note is the same PITCH as taking the next note higher "E" and flatting it to "E♭". We can say, then, that D# = E♭. They are the same pitch (see Ex. 1). "Why?", you may ask. Simply because some KEYS have sharps and only sharps, and some keys have flats and only flats. We will expound on this a little later. By the way, if you want to amaze your friends and be a hit at parties, any two notes with different letter names that are the same pitch (such as D# and E♭), are called ENHARMONIC EQUIVALENTS! In my 27 years in the music biz, I have never needed to use this phrase, but it's so much fun to say!

ANYWAY..... if we write out the musical alphabet with all the enharmonic equivalents (this is the first time, really!!), we get the following twelve notes: A, (A# or B♭), B, C, (C# or D♭), D, (D# or E♭), E, F, (F# or G♭), G, (G# or A♭). Notice that there are twelve notes, the ones in parentheses being enharmonic equivalents or the same pitch. These are all the letter names there are for the notes. There are different octaves of these notes, but the letter names keep repeating. These twelve notes make up a scale called the CHROMATIC SCALE (see Ex.2).

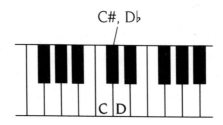

Example 1 - *Here we see that C# and D♭ are the same pitch or* ENHARMONIC EQUIVALENTS.

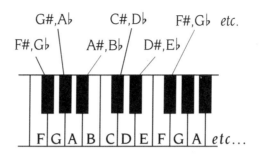

Example 2 - *It's easy to visualize the* CHROMATIC SCALE *on the piano. These are all the notes there are. Notice that after the first 12 notes, the letter names start repeating in another* OCTAVE.

One thing we must take note of (no pun intended), is the fact that since there are no notes between B and C, if we sharp the B (bring it up a half step), we get C. The same thing is true when we sharp an E. We end up on F. This works the same way when flatting a C or F. We get a B or an E, respectively.

In summary, we have covered the following points so far: There are 7 letters in the musical alphabet. They are A, B, C, D, E, F, & G. Remembering that there are no notes between B and C, or between E and F, we can sharp or flat the remaining notes. The result is a scale of 12 notes, each a half step apart. This is called the Chromatic scale. These are all the letter names there are in the musical alphabet!

I strongly suggest that these few basic principles are fully understood before continuing. This will make life in musicland much easier.

Major Scales

CHAPTER TWO

Major Scales

A scale is made up of seven notes. No matter where you start, you will follow the order of the musical alphabet. (Remember that after "G" we start at "A" again.) The only thing to know is how many sharps or flats there are in a scale. The number of sharps or flats there are in a scale is called a KEY SIGNATURE. Every scale has a different key signature. Now if I tell you that the key of "G" has one sharp, and that is an F sharp (F#), then all we have to do is go up the musical alphabet from G to G, and put in the sharp when we come to the F. So the G Major scale would have the following notes: G, A, B, C, D, E, F#, G. That's all there is to it! One thing to keep in mind is that anytime you see a key signature with one sharp, that sharp will ALWAYS be an F#, and it will ALWAYS be the key of "G". The same is true of any other key. Its key signature will be unique. Since we know that there are twelve notes in the chromatic scale, and that we can build a scale from each note, then we see that there are twelve scales, each with its own unique key signature.

Now comes the fun part! How can we easily learn all the key signatures of all the keys? When we see a key signature, how can we instantly tell what key we are in? Firstly, we must realize that all the keys with sharps have ONLY sharps and no flats. Conversely, all the keys with flats have ONLY flats. Secondly, we must realize that there is an order to the sharps and flats. By memorizing the following sequence of seven letters, we can learn ALL the sharps and flats in

ALL the keys. Reading the sequence FORWARDS gives us the order of the sharps. Reading the sequence BACKWARDS gives us the order of the flats! Here we go.........

Order of the Sharps ⟶

F, C, G, D, A, E, B

⟵ Order of the Flats

As I said before, the key of "G" has one sharp, which is an F#. That is the first sharp we see in the list. Keep in mind that each time you add a sharp or flat, you keep the ones before it, too. The next sharp in the list is a C#. Now we have F# and C#. This is the key of "D" (trust me). If we plug these two sharps into the musical alphabet, we see that the notes in the key of "D" are: D, E, F#, G, A, B, C#, D. So, how can we instantly know what key we are in by memorizing the order of the sharps and flats? Here's a simple way of determining the name of the key we are in. For the SHARP KEYS ONLY: THE NAME OF THE KEY IS A HALF STEP ABOVE THE LAST SHARP IN THE KEY SIGNATURE!! For example, let's take another look at the key of "G". It has an F# in the key signature. This is the only sharp in the key signature. Now look at the distance between F# (the last # in this key) and "G" (the name of the key). If we look at the chromatic scale again, we see that F# is a HALF STEP from G. Now let's look at the key of "D" again. As stated previously, the key of "D" has an F# and a C#. The C# is the last sharp in the key signature. What note is a half step above the C#? Of course, it's "D". Then we must be in the key of "D"! Amazing, huh? O.K., let's add the next sharp in the sequence to the ones we already have. If we look at the order of the sharps we see that G# is the next sharp (after F# & C#). So now we have F#, C#, and G#. What note is a half step above the G#? If you guessed "A", you're a regular

Ludwig von!! Now we see that the key of "A" has an F#, C#, and G#. If we put these into the musical alphabet starting on "A" we get: A, B, C#, D, E, F#, G#, and back to A. These are the notes in the A major scale or the key of "A". If we keep doing this with all the sharps as they appear in the order of sharps, we will come to the following revelation:

G   D   A   E   B   F#   C#

Example 3 - *Here we see the SHARP KEYS written on a staff with the names of each key under it. Notice that the last sharp in the key signature is a half step below the name of the key! These are ALL the SHARP keys there are!*

Sharps (#)	Key of
F	G
F,C	D
F,C,G	A
F,C,G,D	E
F,C,G,D,A	B
F,C,G,D,A,E	F#
F,C,G,D,A,E,B	C#

Now let's think backwards for a second. If I asked you what the sharps are in the key of "E", you would have to ask yourself: "What is a half step BELOW an "E"?". By knowing the chromatic scale, we can determine this to be a D#. We would then take all the sharps UP TO and INCLUDING the D#, according to the order of the sharps. This would give us F#, C#, G#, and D#. These are the sharps in the key of "E". (Keep in mind that the reason we use D# and not E♭ when finding the note a half step below E is because we NEVER have two notes that start with the same letter [i.e.: E and E♭] in one scale!!!!).

Now we can tell what key we are in and what sharps are in that key by merely knowing the order of the sharps as shown above. But what about the keys with FLATS? Let's look at the order of the flats. Remember, it is exactly OPPOSITE of the order of sharps: B, E, A, D, G, C, F. The first four of these are the most common. One thing you have to know is that the key of "F" has only one flat, the B♭. Now here's the trick for JUST the FLAT KEYS: THE NEXT TO THE LAST FLAT IN THE KEY SIGNATURE IS THE NAME OF THE KEY YOU ARE IN! This is why you must know that the key of "F" has only a B♭. There is no next to last flat. Now let's add the rest of the flats and see what happens. The next flat in the order is E♭, so now we have a B♭ and an E♭. E♭ is the last flat in this key and B♭ is the next to last. This is also the name of the key we are in: B♭ Major! When we add the next flat in the order, we have B♭, E♭, and A♭. The next to the last flat here is E♭, so we are in the key of E♭! Cosmic!! This is the way we can determine the key signatures for all the flat keys:

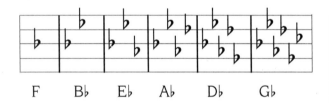

F   B♭   E♭   A♭   D♭   G♭

Flats (♭)	Key of
B	F
B,E	B♭
B,E,A	E♭
B,E,A,D	A♭
B,E,A,D,G	D♭
B,E,A,D,G,C	G♭

Example 4 - *These are all the key signatures of the FLAT keys. Notice that the next to last flat is the name of the key. Notice, also, that the Key of F has only one flat. This is also the only flat key that doesn't have "flat" in its name.*

Take note that here I do not add the F♭ (the last flat in the order). This is because using all seven flats would be the key of C♭, which is the enharmonic equivalent of B. Likewise, the keys of D♭ and G♭ are equivalent to C# and F#, respectively. Notice, also, that all the keys with flats have FLAT (♭) in their name (except for the key of "F"). This will make it easy, when asked a key signature, to determine whether the key has sharps or flats in it.

The foregoing explanation should greatly facilitate the memorization of all the Major Key Signatures. This is most of the memorization you will have to do while learning music theory, but once again, by memorizing these seven letters BACKWARDS and FORWARDS, we can very quickly determine ANY key signature!!

Well..... as they say in the music biz, let's take a pause for the cause, (is it last call, yet?), and review this chapter. So far, we have come to the following conclusions:

1. The key of "C" has no sharps or flats.
2. The key of "F" has one flat: B♭.
3. We must memorize the order of these seven letters backwards and forwards:

    F, C, G, D, A, E, B

4. Reading these forward gives us the order of the sharps.
5. Reading these backward gives us the order of the flats.
6. In the sharp keys, the last sharp is a half step below the name of the key. In the flat keys, the name of the key is the next to the last flat.
7. Each time you add a sharp or flat, you keep the ones before it.
8. To make a Major Scale, we merely go up the musical alphabet, inserting the sharps or flats accordingly (i.e.: the key of "G" has an F# in it, so the notes in the key of "G" are G, A, B, C, D, E, F#, and back to "G".
9. In the music biz, they say "Let's take a pause for the cause."

Chapter 3

Minor Scales

CHAPTER THREE

Minor Scales

This will be a very short chapter. This is because of the fact that THERE IS NO DIFFERENCE BETWEEN A MAJOR AND A MINOR SCALE !!!! "Are you crazy?", you may ask. That's like saying that 2+2 = 4,376,918.25!, or that Superman plays hopscotch!!". Now just calm down. I will prove to you that this is true.

Let's start by taking a C Major scale. Since there are no sharps or flats in this key, we know that the notes in the C Major scale are C, D, E, F, G, A, B, and C. Remember that these notes keep repeating in order, so two OCTAVES of a C MAJOR scale would look like this: C, D, E, F, G, A, B, C, D, E, F, G, A, B, C. (See Ex.5). Now let's find the note THREE LETTER NAMES BEFORE the "C", counting "C" as one. Counting back from "C" we count: (1)"C", (2)"B", (3)"A". As you can see, we end up on the letter "A". Now let's say that we STARTED the scale on "A" and kept the same KEY SIGNATURE as the key of "C" (no sharps or flats). We would get this: A, B, C, D, E, F, G, A (See Ex.6). This is called an A MINOR scale. Notice that it has EXACTLY the same letter names as the key of "C" Major, we're just starting on an "A". Since the "A" Minor scale comes directly from the "C" Major scale, it is called the RELATIVE MINOR to the key of "C".

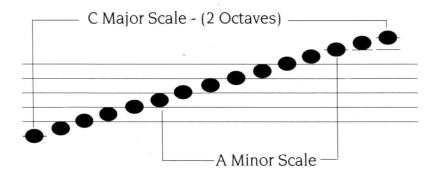

Example 5 & 6 – *The A Minor scale comes directly from the C Major scale, therefore it is called the* RELATIVE MINOR *of C Major. As you can see,* THERE IS NO DIFFERENCE BETWEEN C MAJOR *and* A MINOR *except the starting note!*

We can determine the relative Minor to any Major scale by counting back three letter names from the ROOT of the scale (a ROOT is the first note in the scale and the same letter as the name of the KEY). The key signature of the Major and Relative Minor are exactly the same, but the ROOT is different.

Now let's try another example. Say we wanted to find the Relative Minor to the key of A Major. First, we must determine the key signature of "A". By using the method described in the previous chapter, we find that the key signature for A Major is F#, C#, and G#. Now we know the notes in the key of "A" are: A, B, C#, D, E, F#, G#, and A. We simply count back three letter names from the "A", counting the "A" as one: (1)A, (2)G#, and (3)F#. AHA!! F# must be the Relative Minor to the key of A Major! Now, using the same key signature as the key of A Major, go up the musical alphabet starting on F# (See Ex. 7 & 8). This will give us: F#, G#, A, B, C#, D, E, F#. These are the notes in the key of F# Minor. They are exactly the same as the key of A Major, just starting on F#.

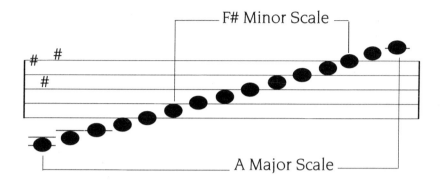

F# Minor Scale

A Major Scale

Example 7 & 8 – *In this example we see an A Major scale (notice the KEY SIGNATURE) and an F# Minor scale. The only difference between these two scales is that they start on different letters of the musical alphabet. The key signature, however, is exactly the same.*

Now let's say that we wanted to find the Relative Major to a Minor scale, say G Minor. We would merely count UP three half steps in the chromatic scale. Starting on "G" we would count: (1) G to G#, (2) G# to A and (3) A to B♭. We MUST use a B♭ instead of an A# because B♭ is three LETTER NAMES away from "G", counting "G" as the first. We will find, now, that G Minor is the same key signature as B♭ Major. Using the method for determining the key signatures as described previously, we see that the key signature for B♭ is B♭ and E♭. This is also the key signature for the key of G Minor. (See Ex.9).

Example 9 - The G Minor Scale

As you can see in Example 9, the key of G Minor has the same key signature as the key of B♭ Major. Both contain exactly the same notes, they just start on different letters of the musical alphabet.

Perhaps now you can understand why I say that there is no difference between Major and Minor scales. For each Major scale there is a minor scale that is related to it. If you have learned all the key signatures for the Major scales, you have also learned all the key signatures for the Minor scales!!! The real difference between the two scales is the MOOD that they create. The Major scale usually conveys a bright or happy mood, while the Minor scale creates a darker, more ominous mood. This can be a useful tool, especially in composing.

Chords

CHAPTER FOUR

Chords

Now that we know all the NOTES in a scale, we can determine all the CHORDS in a scale. To do this, we must further examine INTERVALS. An interval is only the distance between two notes. In naming intervals, the first thing we will do is to see how many letter names apart the two notes are. We can do this by giving each letter name a number. For example, let's look at a G Major scale: G, A, B, C, D, E, F#, and G. Now, starting with the ROOT or the note "G", we will assign each letter a number: G = 1, A = 2, B = 3, C = 4, etc. The letter of each number determines its distance from the first (1) note. The note A is a SECOND interval from G, B is a THIRD from G, C is a FOURTH from G, etc. We can start anywhere in the alphabet and do the same thing. For this chapter, we will mainly be concerned with the interval of a THIRD. Chords are built on intervals of a third that are stacked together. By the way, a CHORD is two or more notes played at the same time. First we will examine chords with only three notes in them. These are called TRIADS. Triads are built with THREE notes, each a THIRD apart.

The interval of a THIRD can have two qualities: it can be a MAJOR THIRD or a MINOR THIRD. This is determined by how many HALF STEPS are in the INTERVAL. A Major third interval is the distance of

FOUR half steps. A Minor third interval is the distance of THREE half steps. For example, let's count the half steps between "G" and "B" (I will not use the enharmonic equivalents). (1) G to G#, (2) G# to A, (3) A to A#, (4) A# to B. AHA!! Here we see that there are 4 half steps between "G" and "B". That means that the distance between "G" and "B" is a MAJOR THIRD interval! (See Ex.11). A MINOR THIRD from G would be a B♭.

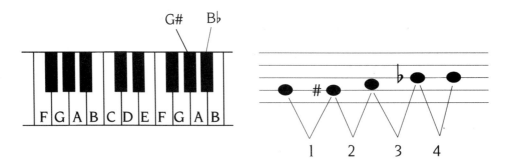

Example 11 – *Here we see that the distance between "G" and "B" is FOUR (4) half steps. This is a MAJOR THIRD interval. The distance between "G" and "B♭", however, is THREE (3) half steps, which is a MINOR THIRD.*

The chords we will be talking about will be built using MAJOR and MINOR THIRD intervals. We will start by building TRIADS, or three note chords. Let's look at the C Major scale, once again, in two octaves.

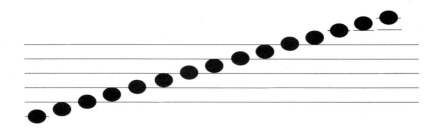

Since there are seven notes in every scale (then they repeat), there will also be seven CHORDS in every scale. Each chord is built on one of the notes in the scale. The note that we build the chord on is called the ROOT of the chord. For example, if we build a chord on the letter "C", then "C" is the root. In a chord built on the letter "D", "D" is the root, etc. Again, all chords are built with a combination of Major and Minor third intervals. Here's an easy way to think of building chords: Whatever note you are building the chord on, take every OTHER note in the scale and stack them on top of the ROOT. This will be a chord built with thirds. Since we are only using three notes in a chord, we only need TWO notes on top of the ROOT. Look at the C Major scale (See Ex. 11). If we started on "C", skipped "D", and added the "E", we have the first interval in the C Major chord: "C" to "E". The "E" note is a MAJOR third from "C", which is the ROOT. It is therefore called the THIRD of the chord. In any chord, the distance from the root of the chord to the third of the chord determines whether the chord is Major or Minor. In this case, the distance from "C" to "E" is a Major third, so the "C" chord will also be a MAJOR CHORD! (See Ex.13). If the distance from the root to the third is a Minor third, the chord will be a MINOR CHORD. Now let's put the next note on the chord. If we start on "E", skip the "F", we end up on "G". Stack this on top of the "C" and the "E" and we will have a C MAJOR TRIAD: C, E, and G. The "G" is called the FIFTH of the chord because that is the distance between "C" and "G". The distance between the "E" and the "G", however, is a MINOR THIRD interval. All Major chords have this relationship, that is: the distance from the root to the third is a Major third interval, and the distance from the third (of the chord) to the fifth is a Minor third interval. I think I confused myself with that one!! To make it easier, a MAJOR CHORD = Maj.3 + Min.3. (See Ex.13b).

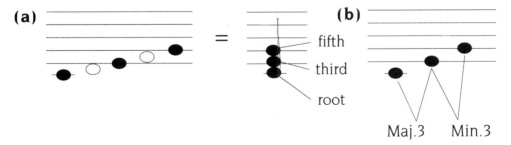

Example 13 – *This shows how we build chords. Starting on "C", we skip the "D", add the "E", skip the "F", and add the "G". This is a C MAJOR TRIAD. "C" is the ROOT, "E" is the THIRD, and*

"G" is the FIFTH. In Ex. 13b, we see that the distance from the ROOT to the third is a MAJOR third interval, and the distance from the third to the fifth is a MINOR third interval. Hence, a MAJOR CHORD = Maj. 3 + Min. 3.

Now let's see what happens when we build a chord on the second note of the C Major scale. This would be the note "D". Using the same method that we used to build the C Major chord, we would find the ROOT of this chord to be a "D", the THIRD of the chord to be an "F", and the FIFTH of this chord to be an "A". Now count the half steps between the ROOT of the chord (D), and the THIRD of the chord (F). You will find that there are three (3) half steps between them. This is a Minor third interval, therefore, the "D" chord is a D Minor chord. (See Ex. 14). Now see how many half steps are between the THIRD (F), and the FIFTH (A). We will find that this is a MAJOR third interval. We can say, then, that a MINOR CHORD = Min.3 + Maj.3.

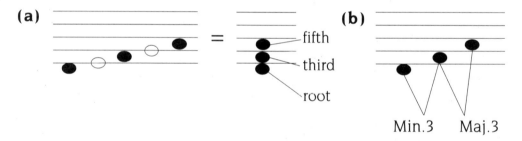

Example 14 - *Again we see how to build a chord, this time starting on a "D" note. Keep in mind that we are still in the key of C Major (no sharps or flats). Since the distance from the ROOT (D), to the THIRD (F) is a Minor third interval, this is a D MINOR CHORD. Ex. 14b shows that a MINOR CHORD = Min.3 + Maj.3.*

So, now we see that when we build a chord off of the "D", which is the second note in the key of "C", we get a D Minor chord, which is also the second CHORD in the key of "C". By now, you should have a good concept of how to build chords. We can build a chord on each of the seven notes in the Major or Minor scales. This will give you seven chords for every scale! Continuing with the C Major scale, we will find that the THIRD chord, built on an "E", is also minor. The notes in the E Minor chord will be "E", "G", and "B". The FOURTH chord, built on "F", is Major, the FIFTH chord, built on "G", is Major, the SIXTH chord, built on "A", is Minor, and the SEVENTH chord, built on "B", is DIMINISHED. (We will talk about this diminished chord shortly.) Now... let's give each chord a roman numeral according to its position in the scale. A capital roman numeral will designate a Major chord, and a small roman numeral will designate a Minor chord. The first chord in the key of C Major is a C Major CHORD, therefore, its roman numeral will be (I). The second chord in this key is D Minor, so its roman numeral will be (ii). Notice that we used a small roman numeral because it is a Minor chord. This will also be true for the third chord, E Minor. Its roman numeral will be (iii). F Major is the fourth chord, so it would be (IV), etc. (See Ex.15).

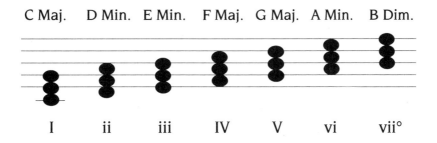

Example 15 – *Here we have determined whether each chord is a Major or Minor by finding the distance between the root and the third of each chord. We then give each chord a roman numeral. Capital numerals show a Major Chord, and small numerals show a minor chord. Notice that the numerals show two things: whether the chord is Major or Minor, and the position of the chord in the scale (i.e. F Major is the fourth chord in the key of C). The Diminished chord (vii) will usually be designated with a small circle (°).*

Let's look at this Diminished chord. In a Diminished chord, ALL THE NOTES ARE A MINOR THIRD AWAY FROM EACH OTHER. Look at the B Dim. chord above. The notes in the chord are B, D, and F. The distance between the "B" and the "D" is a Minor third interval, and the distance between the "D" and the "F" is also a Minor third interval. We can say then, that a DIMINISHED chord = Min.3 + Min. 3. Notice how this is different from the other two types of chords we looked at. (See Ex. 16).

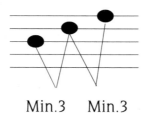

Min.3   Min.3

Example 16 *- The B Diminished chord is built with two Minor third intervals: from the "B" to the "D", and from the "D" to the "F". We can say, then, that a Diminished chord = Min.3 + Min.3.*

Look at the order of the chords again: I, ii, iii, IV, V, vi, and vii dim. Remember that the capital numerals are Major chords, and the small numerals are Minor chords, with the seventh (vii) chord being diminished. This order will be the same in ALL THE MAJOR SCALES!!!! In EVERY Major scale, the first (I) chord is Major, the second (ii) chord is Minor, etc. If you know all the KEY SIGNATURES, then you know all the SCALES. If you know all the SCALES, then you know ALL THE CHORDS IN THE MAJOR KEYS!! Let's try one more key before we take a break. Say we wanted to know all of the chords that are in the key of "F". No problem! By knowing the KEY SIGNATURES we know that the key of "F" has one flat, a B♭. We then know that the notes in the F MAJOR scale are F, G, A, B♭, C, D, E and F. By knowing the notes in the key of "F", we can insert the numerals in the order of the chords to find the CHORDS in the key of F: (I) F Maj., (ii) G Min., (iii) A Min., (IV) B♭ Maj., (V) C Maj., (vi) D Min., and (vii) E Dim. Pretty cool, eh?

Well, let's take a break and look at what we have just discovered:

▲ An INTERVAL is the distance between two notes.

▲ We can determine this distance by how many LETTER NAMES apart they are, counting the first letter as one.

▲ Chords are built with intervals that are a THIRD apart. There are two types of thirds: MAJOR THIRDS (4 half steps apart), and MINOR THIRDS (3 half steps apart).

▲ Right now, we will be dealing with chords that have only THREE notes in them. These chords are called TRIADS.

▲ The first note in a chord is called the ROOT. The middle note is a THIRD, and the top note is a FIFTH.

▲ The distance from the ROOT to the THIRD of a chord determines whether the chord is a MAJOR or a MINOR Chord.

▲ A Major Chord = Maj.3 + Min.3, a Minor Chord = Min.3 + Maj.3, and a Diminished Chord = Min.3 + Min.3.

▲ The order of the chords in a Major Scale is: (I) Maj., (ii) Min., (iii) Min., (IV) Maj., (V) Maj., (vi) Min., (vii) Dim.

Chapter 5

Overview

C H A P T E R   F I V E

Overview, So Far...

Let's take a look at what we should be able to do right now. We should be able to determine ALL the KEY SIGNATURES for ALL of the MAJOR and MINOR SCALES. Let's go through this complete thought process one time. Say we wanted to know everything there is to know about the Key of Eb Major. The first thing we must do is to determine the KEY SIGNATURE for the key of Eb. Firstly, we know that the key signature will have FLATS (not sharps), because the word "flat" is in the name of the key. (Remember, the key of "F" is the only key that has a flat and DOESN'T have flat in its name). Now we look at the ORDER of the FLATS: B, E, A, D, G, C, F . We can determine the flats in the key of Eb by knowing that THE NEXT TO THE LAST FLAT IN THE KEY SIGNATURE IS THE NAME OF THE KEY YOU ARE IN. Sooo..... we know that Eb will be the NEXT TO THE LAST flat in this key signature. This means that when we look at the order of the flats, we need to find the note ONE AFTER the Eb. We see that this is an Ab. Now we will use all the flats UP TO AND INCLUDING the Ab. This gives us: Bb, Eb, and Ab. This is the KEY SIGNATURE for the key of Eb. Knowing this, we can go up the MUSICAL ALPHABET to determine the NOTES in the key of Eb Major: Eb, F, G, Ab, Bb, C, D, and Eb. This is the Eb MAJOR SCALE. Now that we have the NOTES in the scale, we can build CHORDS on each of the notes to get the CHORDS in the scale. By using the ORDER of the CHORDS and merely inserting the NUMERALS accordingly, we find that the CHORDS IN THE KEY OF

E♭ are: (I) E♭ Maj., (ii) F Min., (iii) G Min., (IV) A♭ Maj., (V) B♭ Maj., (vi) C Min., and (vii) D Dim.

Notice that we completed this whole process by knowing THREE things:
▲ The first seven letters of the alphabet.
▲ The order of the sharps and flats.
▲ The order of the chords in a scale.

That's all there is to it!! We can now figure out ALL THE KEY SIGNATURES FOR ALL THE MAJOR AND MINOR SCALES as well as ALL THE CHORDS that go with them. WAY COOL!!!! The rest of this book will deal with variations of this line of thought. It is imperative, therefore, that you fully understand everything up to here before going any further!

Chapter 6

Chords in the Minor Scales

CHAPTER SIX

Chords in the Minor Scales

As we have seen, the Minor scale and its relative Major have the same key signature and the same notes. The only difference is the NUMERICAL POSITION of these notes. This will also be true with the CHORDS in the Minor scales. The chords of the Minor scale will be EXACTLY the same as those of its Relative Major. The only difference will be the NUMERICAL POSITION of the chords. Since the RELATIVE MINOR of ANY MAJOR scale starts on the SIXTH note, the FIRST chord of a MINOR scale will be the same as the SIXTH CHORD of its RELATIVE MAJOR. (See Ex.17 & 18).

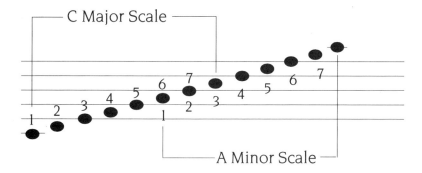

Example 17– *Here we see that C Major and A Minor contain the same notes, but the NUMERICAL POSITION is the only thing that changes. This will also be true with the CHORDS. Obviously, if we are using the same group of notes, we will get the same group of CHORDS.*

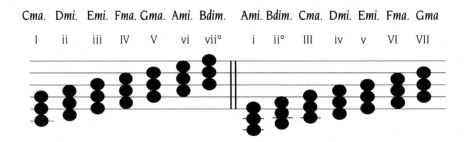

Example 18 - *The Chords in the key of* C Major *are the same as the chords in the key of* A Minor, *except for the numerical position.*

Seventh Chords

CHAPTER SEVEN

Seventh Chords

So far, we have been dealing with chords that have three notes in them, called TRIADS. These triads are the foundation of all other types of chords. In other words, all the other types of chords that we will be discussing will be built on these triads. When building on these triads, we do the same thing that we did to build the triads, that is, we keep stacking up THIRD INTERVALS. So far, we have started on a ROOT note, added the THIRD to the chord, then added the FIFTH on top of that. This is your basic, everyday triad. The note that is a third interval above the FIFTH of the chord is called a SEVENTH. It is called this because that is the distance it is from the ROOT of the chord. (See Ex.19). An easier way to think of SEVENTHS is to ask yourself : "What letter comes right before the root in the alphabet ?". Let's take the key of C Major again. (AGAIN?! Yeah, I already have it drawn out!). C, D, E, F, G, A, B, and C. Look familiar? Now if we look back at Ex.17, we see that if we start on "C", the "B" is SEVEN letter names away. It is the SEVENTH of "C". This is the note we will add to the C MAJOR CHORD. When we add this note, we will have : C, E, G, and B. This is called a C Maj.7 chord. Notice that the "B" note is the note right before "C" in the musical alphabet. It's just easier to think of it this way rather than counting up seven letters from "C".

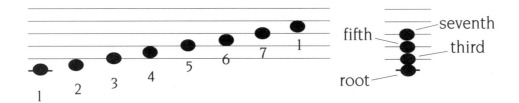

Example 19 – *The "B" note is a* SEVENTH *interval from the* ROOT *(C). Notice, also, that it is a half step away from "C". When finding* SEVENTHS, *ask yourself: "What letter name comes right* BEFORE *the* ROOT?" *In this case, the "B" is the letter right before "C" in the alphabet. Remember, also, to stay in the* KEY. *The chord above is called a* C MAJOR SEVENTH CHORD *and is usually written as "C Maj. 7". A Major Seventh chord is a Major triad with a* SEVENTH *that is a* HALF STEP *from the* ROOT.

As we see in Example 19, a MAJOR SEVENTH chord is a Major triad with a SEVENTH added to it. This SEVENTH is a HALF STEP from the ROOT. This is just one kind of SEVENTH chord. For example, let's look at the D Minor chord, the second (ii) chord in the key of "C". The notes in a D Min. chord are D, F, and A. We can determine what the SEVENTH of this chord is by asking ourselves: "What letter comes before "D" in the alphabet?". Remember to stay in the key of C Major. We will find this note to be a "C". If we add this to the D Minor triad, we will have D, F, A, and C. Notice that now the SEVENTH is a WHOLE STEP from the root and the TRIAD is a MINOR chord. This is called a MINOR SEVENTH chord. (See Ex.20).

Now let's take a look at the G Major chord. This is the fifth (V) chord in the key of C Major. What letter comes right before "G" in the key of "C"? Of course, it's "F". When we add this note to the G Major triad we have G, B, D, and F. Notice that in this chord, the SEVENTH (F) is a WHOLE STEP from the ROOT (G). Now we have a chord where the TRIAD is a MAJOR triad and the SEVENTH is a WHOLE STEP from the ROOT. This is called a DOMINANT SEVENTH chord. (See Ex.20).

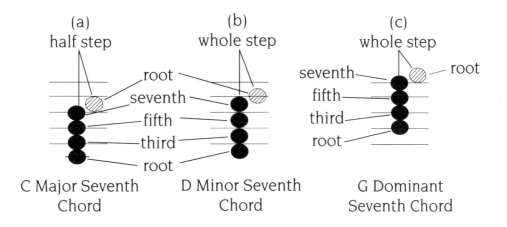

C Major Seventh Chord   D Minor Seventh Chord   G Dominant Seventh Chord

Example 20 – (a) - *Here we see the construction of a C Major Seventh chord. Most of the time you will see it written as "C Maj.7". Notice that the SEVENTH of the chord (B) is a HALF STEP away from the ROOT (C).*

(b) - Here is a D Minor Seventh chord, usually written as "Dm7". This is a MINOR chord where the SEVENTH (C) of the chord is a WHOLE STEP from the ROOT (D).

(c) - This is a G Dominant Seventh chord, usually written as "G7". Like the "C" chord, this is a Major TRIAD. The difference here is that the SEVENTH (F) is a WHOLE STEP from the root (G).

All the chords here are in the key of C Major. C Maj.7 is the first (I) chord, Dm7 is the second (ii) chord, and G7 is the fifth (V) chord in the key of C Major.

So far, we know this about SEVENTH CHORDS:

A MAJOR TRIAD + a SEVENTH that is a HALF STEP from the ROOT is called a MAJOR SEVENTH chord (Maj.7).

A MAJOR TRIAD + a SEVENTH that is a WHOLE STEP from the ROOT is called a DOMINANT SEVENTH chord (7).

A MINOR TRIAD + a SEVENTH that is a WHOLE STEP from the ROOT is called a MINOR SEVENTH chord (m7).

These are the three types of chords in the Major and Minor scales with the exception of the DIMINISHED chord. We know that the diminished TRIAD consists of notes that are all a MINOR THIRD away from each other. Look at the last chord (vii) in the key of "C". We see that it is a B Diminished chord. The notes in the TRIAD are B, D, and F. From the "B" to the "D" is a Minor third, and the "D" to the "F" is a Minor third. When we add the seventh to this triad, we find this note to be an "A". Now, what is the distance between "F" and "A"? By counting the HALF STEPS, we see that this is a MAJOR THIRD. This chord cannot be a true DIMINISHED chord, then. There are a couple of names for this chord, depending on whether you're in jazz land or in classical land. For now, we will call this a HALF DIMINISHED chord, (classical). Its symbol is a circle with a slash through it ($^\phi$). (See Ex.21).

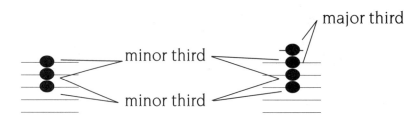

B Diminished Triad (°)   B Half Diminished chord ($^\phi$)

Example 21– *The example on the left shows a DIMINISHED triad. The intervals are both a MINOR third apart. When we add the SEVENTH to the triad, the distance between the FIFTH of the chord (F) and the SEVENTH of the chord (A) is a MAJOR third interval. This is what we call a HALF DIMINISHED chord.*

So, now we see that there are four kinds of Seventh chords in the Major and Minor scales: a MAJOR SEVENTH, a MINOR SEVENTH, a DOMINANT SEVENTH, and a HALF DIMINISHED chord. The Half Diminished chord is also called a MINOR SEVENTH FLAT FIVE chord, (jazz terminology), min.7♭5 or m7♭5. This is because this chord is a Minor Seventh chord with the FIFTH being FLATTED or lowered a half step. This is the name we will use for this chord from now on.

Now let's go back to the formula for the chords in a Major scale (I, ii, iii IV, V, vi, and vii°) and add the SEVENTHS to all the chords. We will stay in the key of C Major. The first chord (I) would be a C Major Seventh (C Maj.7) chord, the second chord will be a D Minor Seventh (Dm7) chord, the third chord is an E Minor Seventh (Em7) chord, the fourth chord is an F Major Seventh (F Maj.7) chord, the fifth chord is a G Dominant Seventh (G7), the sixth chord is an A Minor Seventh (Am7), and the seventh chord is a B Minor Seven flat five or B half diminished (Bm7♭5) chord.

I	ii	iii	IV	V	vi	vii$^{\o}$
Cmaj7	Dm7	Em7	Fmaj7	G7	Am7	Bm7♭5

Example 22– *Here we see the ORDER of the CHORDS in a MAJOR scale with the SEVENTHS added to all the chords. Keep in mind that this order will be the same for ALL the scales. We just used C Major for the example here. Notice that the (V) chord, (in this case, G7), is the ONLY chord in the scale that is a DOMINANT SEVENTH chord. The (I) and the (IV) chords are both Major seventh chords, the (ii), (iii), and (vi) chords are all Minor seventh chords, and the (vii) chord is a type of a Minor seventh chord. The (V) is the only DOMINANT chord.*

Chord Progressions

CHAPTER EIGHT

Chord Progressions

Let's look at what we can do NOW!!!

- We can determine all the KEY SIGNATURES for ALL the Major and Minor scales by knowing the ORDER of the SHARPS and FLATS.
- By knowing all the MAJOR scales, we also know all the MINOR scales.
- We can determine the CHORDS in all the MAJOR scales by knowing the FORMULA for chords in the Major scale.
- We know the CHORDS in the MINOR scales by merely changing the NUMERIC POSITION of these chords.

In other words, we can figure out ALL the key signatures and ALL the scales and ALL the chords in EVERY key!!! Now, how many of you are saying "So what!!", "What does it all mean?!", "What good does it do?". Let's see a show of hands. UH-HUH!! I thought so. Once again, allow me to elucidate. Songs are made up of two elements, basically: a MELODY, which is the part you whistle while you're walking down the street, and the CHORDS that the melody is played over. These chords in a song can determine the HARMONY to be used, the KEY of the song, and any KEY CHANGES that will happen in the song, as well as the overall MOOD of the song. As you can see, these chords effect many elements of the song. The way the chords are put together, or the order of the chords in a song, is called a CHORD PROGRESSION. By knowing the chords in a key, we can easily put together our own chord progressions or we can look at a song and tell what key we're in. All these things are very important if you want to compose a song. For example, say you wanted to write a song in the key of G Major. Here are the thought processes you would go through: First, you would find the KEY SIGNATURE for the key of G Major. By using the ORDER of the SHARPS and FLATS, you will see that the key of "G" has one sharp, an F# (see Ex. 24a), so we know that the notes in the key of G Major are: G, A, B, C, D, E, F#, G. Now by knowing the ORDER of the CHORDS in a Major scale, we see that the chords in the key of G Major are: G Maj.7 (I), Am7 (ii), Bm7(iii), C Maj.7 (IV), D7 (V), Em7 (vi), and F#m7♭5 (vii). (See Ex. 24b).

Example 24a– *By knowing the order of the sharps, we know that the key of G Major has an F# in the key signature, so the notes in the key of G are: G, A, B, C, D, E, F#, G.*

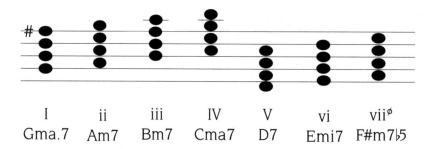

I	ii	iii	IV	V	vi	vii⌀
Gma.7	Am7	Bm7	Cma7	D7	Emi7	F#m7♭5

Example 24b – *By knowing the order of the chords in a Major scale, we see that the chords in the key of G Major are: G Maj.7 (I), Am7 (ii), Bm7 (iii), C Maj.7 (IV), D7 (V), Em7 (vi), and F#m7♭5 (vii). Notice that the fifth (V) chord is the only chord that is a DOMINANT seventh.*

By knowing the CHORDS in the key of G Major, we can put together a group of chords into a CHORD PROGRESSION. For this example, let's say that each chord will be played for two measures each, and that each measure will have four beats in it (4/4 time). Each chord then, would be held out for eight beats. Let's also say that we will use four chords from the key of G Major in our progression. Let's try the (I) chord, the (vi) chord, the (IV) chord, and the (V) chord. In other words, the G Ma7, Em7, C Ma7, and the D7 chords. Sometimes, especially in jazz, you will see CHORD CHARTS written that do not have a melody, just chords. They will usually look something like this:

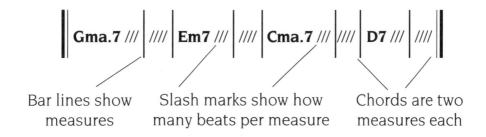

Bar lines show measures   Slash marks show how many beats per measure   Chords are two measures each

Example 25 – A CHORD CHART *shows the CHORD PROGRESSION of a song. The double bars show the beginning and ending of a section. Notice that the notation of the chord counts as one beat, so there are only three slash marks in the measures that have chord names in them. Each chord is held for eight beats (four beats per measure, two measures each).*

Now that we have a chord progression, we can put a MELODY to it. Since all of the chords are in the key of G Major, we can create a melody using the G Major SCALE. The two main components of writing a good melody are the INTERVALS between the notes and the PHRASING of the notes. The phrasing refers to the length of each note. Given just these two variables, the combinations are endless. In my opinion, you can use any note over any chord and theoretically justify it. It depends on the MOOD that you want to convey. Again, the possibilities are limitless. Also, because of the fact that there are FOUR notes in every chord, and there are SEVEN notes in the scale, there are always THREE notes in the scale that are not in the chord. These notes will be different depending on the chord. In the G Maj.7 chord, for example, the notes are G, B, D, and F#. This leaves the A, C, and E. When played over the G Maj.7 chord, these notes are called PASSING TONES. This is because they pass between two notes that ARE in the chord (See Ex. 26). As you can see, it is necessary to know the notes in the chords. This should come easily if you have studied the last chapter. Using this method, it is really impossible to hit a WRONG note, although some notes may sound better than others. This is your personal choice. With PASSING TONES, however, the one that sounds the most awkward is the note that is a FOURTH away from the ROOT of the chord. (See Ex. 27). This note creates a very UNRESOLVED sound, like it should go somewhere. When it *is* resolved, though, it creates a nice tension and release.

I know that these are very abstract thoughts that might not make very much sense right now, but these concepts are the basis of composition and improvisation. You should start becoming aware of these things.

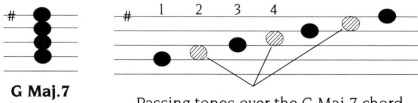

G Maj.7

Passing tones over the G Maj.7 chord

Example 26 & 27 – *On the left we see the notes in the G Maj.7 chord (G, B, D, and F#). On the right we see the notes in the chord with the PASSING TONES being the lightly shaded notes. These are the notes that are NOT in the G Maj.7 chord. The FOURTH note (C) from the ROOT (G) will create TENSION in the chord unless it is RESOLVED or released. (This note is usually resolved to the note before it, in this case the "B".)*

Now try writing a MELODY over this CHORD PROGRESSION. Once again, the possibilities are limitless given the different timing and phrasing combinations. Right now, there are no hard core rules, except staying in the key. By following these few simple concepts, you can write a melody, never actually hearing it, and know it will sound cool! It is IMPOSSIBLE to hit a WRONG note!!! After awhile, you will develop an ear for the things YOU like to hear. You will then be able to convey those thoughts on paper. This is the beginning of accomplishing our goal.

One more thought before we take a break here.... because of the fact that we are thinking of scales, notes, and chords as NUMBERS in relation to each other, it is now much easier to TRANSPOSE something from one key to another. Let's look at our progression again: G Maj.7, Em7, C Maj.7 and D7. We know that these are the (I), (vi), (IV), and (V) chords in the key of G Major. Well, let's say that the girl singer wants to sing it in E♭ (see how they are). All we would have to do, then, is to find the (I), (vi), (IV), and (V) chords in the key of E♭. This would give us E♭ Maj.7, Cm7, A♭ Maj.7 and B♭7. We will go into much more detail about these things when we study composition and jazz improvisation. For now, though, I think it is important to start thinking this way.

Harmonic Minor Scales

CHAPTER NINE

Harmonic Minor Scales

A HARMONIC MINOR scale is merely a NATURAL Minor scale with the SEVENTH note SHARPED or raised a half step. Take another look at the A Minor scale. First, we know, that by counting up three (3) half steps from "A", we end up on "C". We know then that the key of A Minor and C Major will have the same key signature, so the key of A Minor will have no sharps or flats. The notes in the key of A Minor would therefore be: A, B, C, D, E, F, and G. The seventh note is "G". If we make it a G#, we will have: A, B, C, D, E, F, and G#. This is an "A" HARMONIC MINOR scale. (See Ex. 29). This scale has a very Spanish sound to it. Some people refer to it as a Gypsy Minor scale.

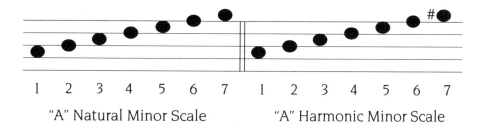

| 1 | 2 | 3 | 4 | 5 | 6 | 7 | 1 | 2 | 3 | 4 | 5 | 6 | 7 |

"A" Natural Minor Scale   "A" Harmonic Minor Scale

Example 29 – *If we take a NATURAL MINOR scale and SHARP the seventh note, we have a HARMONIC MINOR scale. This produces a Spanish or gypsy-like sound.*

Even though there is only one note difference between these two scales, there is a profound difference in their tonality and the mood that they create. This can be seen and heard easily if we examine the CHORDS that are created in the Harmonic Minor scale. To do this, we will need to go back and look at the chords in the "A" (natural) Minor scale again. They are:

i) Am7, (ii) Bm7♭5, (III) C Ma.7, (iv) Dm7, (v) Em7, (VI) F Ma.7, and (VII) G7. (See Ex. 30).

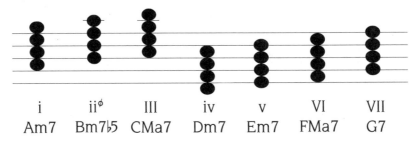

Example 30– *Here are the chords in the* **"A" Natural Minor** *scale. Notice that these are the same chords that are in the key of C Major, except that the numerical position has changed. In the HARMONIC MINOR scale, the only difference is the G# instead of G. Look at the profound difference in the chords that this creates.*

Let's add the G# to all the chords in this key that have a "G" in them. This will be every OTHER chord in the scale, so the (ii), (iv), and (VI) chord will remain unchanged. The difference will be in the (i), (III), (v) and the (VII) chords. We will discuss each one individually. The first chord in the natural minor scale is Am7. The notes in this chord are A, C, E, and G. In the HARMONIC MINOR scale, however, the "G" would change to a "G#". This would give us A, C, E, and G#. As you can see, the TRIAD of the chord is a regular Minor chord, but the SEVENTH (G#) is a HALF STEP from the ROOT (A), making it a MAJOR SEVENTH. (See Ex. 31). What could this possibly be? What do you call this? Well, actually it is called exactly what it is: a Minor/Maj.7 chord. You may see this written as Am/Maj.7.

G# is a half step
from the root (A)

Example 31– *The first chord in the "A" Harmonic Minor scale is an Am / Maj.7 chord. The TRIAD (A, C, E) is a normal minor chord. The SEVENTH, however, is a half step from the ROOT, making it a MAJOR SEVENTH. I call this a "soap opera" chord because it is usually used during a tense moment.*

This is the first chord in the "A" HARMONIC MINOR scale. It creates a very suspenseful sound, almost eerie but unresolved.

Now let's look at the THIRD chord in this scale. Changing the "G" to a "G#", we would have C, E, G#, and B. Following the rules for chord construction, we see that the distance from the ROOT (C) to the THIRD (E), is a Major third interval. This must be some kind of Major chord then, right? Not exactly. See.... there's that darned G# again, screwing everything up. We see that the distance between the THIRD (E) and the FIFTH (G#) is ALSO a Major third. Now we have two Major third intervals in this triad. This is called an AUGMENTED chord. (See Ex. 32a). In a true AUGMENTED chord, ALL the notes are a MAJOR third away from each other, or, an AUGMENTED chord = Maj.3 + Maj.3. Now look at the distance between the FIFTH (G#) and the SEVENTH (B) of the chord. Hey! That's not a Major third, it's a Minor third!! (I knew you were thinking that.) Well, then, this must NOT be a true AUGMENTED chord. This is called an AUGMENTED SEVENTH chord. (See Ex. 32b).

A true Augmented chord has all Major third intervals.

An Augmented seventh chord has an Augmented TRIAD with the seventh being a Minor third from the FIFTH.

Example 32a & 32b – *Example 32a shows a true AUGMENTED chord. Notice that if we went up a Major third from the G#, we would end up on C again. For this reason, there can only be three notes in a true AUGMENTED chord. Example 32b shows the same chord with a B note on top. This is an AUGMENTED SEVENTH chord. Notice that the B is also a half step from the ROOT (C).*

The AUGMENTED SEVENTH chord also has a dissonant and unresolved sound. It sounds similar to the Min./Maj.7 chord. Perhaps this is because the top three notes of a Min./Maj.7 chord make up an augmented triad (i.e., the top three notes of the Am/Maj.7 chord are C, E, and G# !).

Now let's see what happens when we add the G# to the FIFTH chord in the "A" Harmonic Minor scale, or the E chord. We will get the following notes: E, G#, B, and D. You should recognize this as a plain old, every day, DOMINANT SEVENTH chord! AHA!! The FIFTH chord in the HARMONIC MINOR scale is a DOMINANT chord just like in the MAJOR scale. This is one of the main uses of this scale: to play in a Minor key and have the FIFTH chord be DOMINANT. (Notice in the Natural Minor scale the fifth chord is a minor seventh.) So the FIFTH (V) chord of the "A" HARMONIC MINOR scale is an E7 chord.

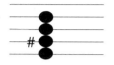

A plain, old E Dominant
Seventh (E7) chord

Example 33– *The FIFTH chord of an A HARMONIC MINOR scale is an E7 chord. Having the FIFTH (V) chord be a dominant chord in a minor scale is one of the main uses of the Harmonic Minor scale.*

Finally, let's look at the SEVENTH chord in the key of "A" Harmonic Minor. Here we see that the notes in this chord will be G#, B, D, and F. The distance from the ROOT (G#) to the THIRD (B) is a Minor third, from the THIRD (B) to the FIFTH (D) is a Minor third, from the FIFTH to the SEVENTH is another Minor third. Heck!! They're ALL Minor third intervals. No shortage of Minor thirds here! This is a true DIMINISHED chord. ALL THE NOTES ARE A MINOR THIRD APART!! The difference between this chord and the m7♭5 (or half diminished) chord, is that the m7♭5 chord has a MAJOR third interval between the FIFTH and the SEVENTH.

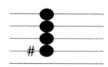

G# Diminished chord
(G#°)

Example 34 – *The seventh chord in the "A" HARMONIC MINOR scale is a G# Diminished. It is a true Diminished chord because ALL the notes are a Minor third apart from each other.*

The rest of the chords in the "A" Harmonic Minor scale (ii, iv, and VI) will be the same as in the natural Minor scale. This is because the G# does not affect these chords. Example 35 shows all the chords in the "A" HARMONIC MINOR scale. One other thing to look at is the fact that the Harmonic Minor scale is the ONLY scale where the FIFTH

(V) and SIXTH (VI) chords are BOTH MAJOR chords and they are only a HALF STEP APART from each other. This is where a lot of Spanish sounding music comes from!

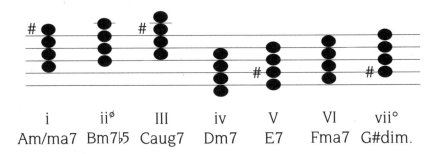

i	ii⌀	III	iv	V	VI	vii°
Am/ma7	Bm7♭5	Caug7	Dm7	E7	Fma7	G#dim.

Example 35– *Here are all the chords in the "A" HARMONIC MINOR scale. Notice that the FIVE (V) chord is a DOMINANT SEVENTH chord, also the (V) and (VI) chords are both Major chords and they are a half step apart from each other. These are some of the things that create the unique sound of the HARMONIC MINOR scale!*

In review, a HARMONIC MINOR scale is a Natural Minor scale with the SEVENTH note of that scale being SHARPED or raised a half step. This creates unique characteristics in the chords of this scale. First, we have a MINOR scale where the FIFTH (V) chord is a DOMINANT SEVENTH chord, and, secondly, we have two chords (the V and VI chords) that are a half step apart, yet both are MAJOR chords. Even though the (V) chord is a DOMINANT seventh and the VI chord is a MAJOR seventh, the TRIADS of these chords are both MAJOR. This is my all time favorite scale!!

Melodic Minor Scales

CHAPTER TEN

Melodic Minor Scales

The MELODIC MINOR scale has two parts: the ASCENDING (going up) part, and the DESCENDING (going down) part. Let's look at the DESCENDING part first. The descending part of the MELODIC MINOR scale is a NATURAL Minor scale. Need I say more? No need to elucidate here. It's just a regular old, plain, vanilla MINOR scale. O.K., now let's look at the ASCENDING part of the MELODIC MINOR scale. In the ascending part, we take the NATURAL Minor scale and SHARP the SIXTH and SEVENTH notes. Let's take "A" Minor, again. The notes in this scale are: A, B, C, D, E, F, G, and A. The sixth and seventh notes are F and G. When we SHARP these, the "A" Melodic Minor scale will look like this: A, B, C, D, E, F#, G# and A. (See Ex.36). So a MELODIC MINOR scale is a Natural Minor scale where we SHARP the SIXTH and SEVENTH when we're ASCENDING, and use a NATURAL Minor scale when we're DESCENDING. What!!! Why would anybody want to do that!!? Well... it's just a compositional tool. Look at the ASCENDING part again. Notice that it is almost the same as an "A" MAJOR scale. The only difference is the THIRD note of the scale, in this case, "C". In the Major scale, the C is sharped, but in the MELODIC MINOR scale the C is NATURAL. An easy way to think of the ASCENDING part of the MELODIC MINOR scale is to think of it as a MAJOR SCALE WITH A FLATTED THIRD .

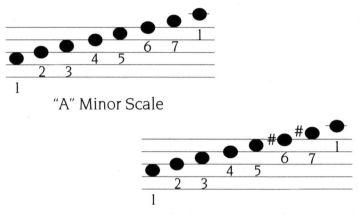

"A" Minor Scale

"A" Melodic Minor Scale (ascending)

"A" Major Scale

Example 36– By SHARPING *the* SIXTH *and* SEVENTH *of the* NATURAL *minor scale, we get a* MELODIC MINOR *scale (ascending). Notice that the only difference between the Melodic minor and the Major scale is the THIRD note, in this case, "C". It is a C natural in the Melodic minor, but a C sharp in the Major scale.*

Now let's look at the entire MELODIC MINOR scale. Remember, when it is ascending, you SHARP the SIXTH and the SEVENTH notes. When it is descending, it is the same as a NATURAL MINOR scale.

The entire MELODIC MINOR scale

In much of today's music, jazz for example, only the ASCENDING part of this scale is used. Let's look at the chords created by this scale. The FIRST chord is A, C, E, and G#. You may recognize this as an Am/Maj.7 chord. This is the first chord in the Harmonic Minor scale, also. The SECOND chord is B, D, F#, and A. This is a regular, old, Minor Seventh chord, in this case, a Bm7. The THIRD chord in this scale is C, E, G#, and B. Again, this is the same as the third chord in the Harmonic Minor scale, a Caug.7 chord. The FOURTH chord is D, F#, A, and C. This is a Dominant Seventh chord, a D7. Yowza!!! ... A DOMINANT chord that is not the FIFTH of the scale! This is one of the more interesting attributes of the MELODIC MINOR scale. The FIFTH chord is E, G#, B, and D, or an E7 chord. Can this be true? TWO dominant chords in one scale!! I told you this was a weird scale. The SIXTH chord is F#, A, C, and E. We see that this is an F#m7♭5 (or F#∅) chord. Finally, the SEVENTH chord in this scale is G#, B, D, and F#. Now, wait a second... can it be?... it is !!! Another Minor Seven Flat Five chord, a Gm7♭5!! Now let's see what we have:

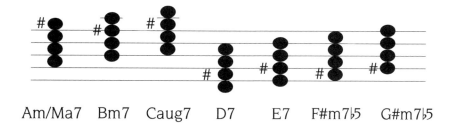

Am/Ma7   Bm7   Caug7   D7   E7   F#m7♭5   G#m7♭5

Example 36a – *The MELODIC MINOR scale has TWO DOMINANT chords right next to each other, the (IV) and the (V) chords. There are also TWO Minor Seven Flat Five chords, the (vi) and the (vii) chords.*

Chapter 11

Blues Scales

CHAPTER ELEVEN

Blues Scales

The scales we have talked about so far each have a particular set of rules and stuff.   This is NOT true with the blues scales. These scales have one primary purpose in life: to PLAY THE BLUES. First let's look at what the BLUES are. The blues are mainly based on a CHORD PROGRESSION that stems from the ONE (I), the FOUR (IV), and the FIVE (V) chord of a Major scale. Say we are in the key of C Major, these chords would be C (I), F (IV), and G (V). The strange thing about the blues, however, is that ALL the chords are DOMINANT SEVENTH chords! The chords in a typical C BLUES progression would be C7, F7, and G7. The following example is of a 12 bar blues in the key of C.

‖ C7/// | F7/// | C7/// | //// | F7/// | //// | C7/// | //// |

G7/// | F7/// | C7/// | G7/// ‖

Example 37 – *This is a typical BLUES PROGRESSION in the key of C. Notice that it consists of the (I), (IV), and (V) chord in the key of C, but* ALL THE CHORDS ARE DOMINANT SEVENTH CHORDS!!

Well, now ..... what do we do with this? When trying to create melodies over this progression, it is helpful to know the BLUES SCALE. It is not like anything we've studied so far. The easiest way to explain this is to just show you what it looks like. Here is the C Blues scale. Notice the distances between each note!

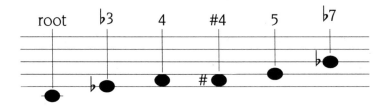

Example 38 – *One way to think of the BLUES SCALE is to see the distance each note is from the root. You could also look at the intervals between the notes, for example, the E♭ is a Minor third from the C, etc.*

Whichever method you use to learn the BLUES SCALES, it will be well worth the time. Make sure to learn them in ALL THE KEYS!!!! This will take some time, but will become EXTREMELY useful when examining improvisational techniques or just PLAYING THE BLUES!

Test 1 : Basics & Major Scales

1. What letter comes after "G" in the Musical Alphabet?
2. What is the smallest distance that you can have between two notes?
3. What does it mean to (a) SHARP a note? (b) FLAT a note?
4. What is an INTERVAL?
5. Two notes with the same PITCH that are different LETTER NAMES are called _____.
6. What is the CHROMATIC SCALE?
7. What is a KEY SIGNATURE?
8. What is the ORDER of the SHARPS? FLATS?
9. Name the SHARPS or FLATS for the following keys: F, G, Bb, A, E, F#.
10. (Extra credit question) In the music biz, they say "Let's take a

_____.

Test 2 : Minor Scales

1. What is the difference between a Major and a Minor scale? Why is this true?
2. How do we determine the RELATIVE MINOR scale from a Major scale?
3. How do we determine the RELATIVE MAJOR scale from the Minor scale?
4. Name the RELATIVE MINOR scales to the following Major scales: A, D, Eb, G, Bb, C, E.
5. Name the RELATIVE MAJOR scales to the following Minor scales: A, D, E, F#, C#, Bb, C.

Test 3 : Chords

1. How do we determine the distance of an interval?
2. What is a CHORD?
3. What intervals do we use to build chords?
4. How many half steps are these intervals?
5. What is a TRIAD?
6. What are the ROOT, the THIRD and the FIFTH of a chord?
7. What is the formula for a MAJOR chord? MINOR chord? DIMINISHED chord?
8. What is the formula for the CHORDS IN A MAJOR SCALE?
9. Name all the CHORDS in the following KEYS: D, E♭, B, F, E.

Test 4 : Chords in the Minor Scale

1. What is the only difference between a MAJOR scale and its RELATIVE MINOR?
2. What is the formula for CHORDS IN THE MINOR SCALE?
3. Name all the chords in the following MINOR scales: G, A, F, D, E♭, C#.
4. What is the difference in SOUND between the MAJOR and MINOR scales?

Test 5 : Seventh Chords

1. How do we determine the interval of a SEVENTH in a chord?
2. An easy way to think of the SEVENTH of a chord is to ask yourself : _____?
3. What is a MAJOR SEVENTH chord?
4. What is a MINOR SEVENTH chord?
5. What is a DOMINANT SEVENTH chord?

6. Where do we find the DOMINANT SEVENTH chord in a Major scale (numerically)?
7. What is the ORDER of the CHORDS in a Major scale once we add the SEVENTHS?

Test 6 : *Chord Progressions*

1. What are the two basic elements that make up a song?
2. Name three things that the CHORDS in a song can determine.
3. What is the ORDER of the CHORDS in a song called?
4. What is a CHORD CHART?
5. What is a PASSING TONE?
6. If we are playing a GMa7 chord, what note in the G Major scale sounds "unresolved"?
7. What are the I, vi, ii, and V chords in the following keys: G, C, A♭, F, D?

Test 7 : *Harmonic Minor Scales*

1. How do we make a HARMONIC MINOR scale?
2. What is the ORDER of the CHORDS in the Harmonic Minor scale?
3. What intervals make up a Minor/Major7 (Min./Ma7) chord?
4. What is the difference between an AUGMENTED and AUGMENTED SEVENTH chord?
5. The V chord becomes a _____ chord again in the Harmonic Minor scale.
6. In the Harmonic Minor scale, which chords are a half step apart and also both Major chords?

Test 8 : Melodic Minor Scales

1. How do we make a MELODIC MINOR scale?
2. What is the ORDER of the CHORDS in a MELODIC MINOR scale?
3. What is the difference between a MELODIC MINOR (ascending) scale and a MAJOR scale?
4. What is the difference between the DESCENDING MELODIC MINOR scale and a MINOR scale?
5. Which chords are DOMINANT chords in the Melodic Minor scale?
6. Which chords are m7♭5 (or half diminished) chords in the Melodic Minor scale?

INDEX

NOTES

NOTES

NOTES

NOTES

NOTES

NOTES

NOTES

NOTES

NOTES

NOTES

NOTES

NOTES

NOTES

NOTES